Picking Scabs from the Body History

Joanne Godley

A Publication of The Poetry Box®

Poems ©2020 Joanne Godley
All rights reserved.

Editing & Book Design: Shawn Aveningo Sanders
Cover Photo: Timothy Unobeji

No part of this book may be reproduced in any manner whatsoever without permission from the author, except in the case of brief quotations embodied in critical essays, reviews and articles.

ISBN: 978-1-948461-63-4
Printed in the United States of America.
Wholesale Distribution via Ingram.

Published by The Poetry Box®, 2020
Portland, Oregon
ThePoetryBox.com

"To be a Negro in this country and to be relatively conscious is to be in a rage almost all the time."

—*James Baldwin*

I

Lead her to the water's edge to drink from word composition
    cocoons harboring information
wisdom fountains infusing
indelible truths / nourishment
shielding / molding / guiding
pages as staircases
essays as revelations

O great library
this nine-year-old brown girl courtesies at your En~Trance
    show her
the Way
reveal naked Truths
clear awkward ancestral paths
allow her to taste / sample / feel
then   revel in
Herstory

in Books

II

a black and white picture horror book*
bristles the hair on my fearful arms
I turn page after curious page   of photos
gentile outdoor social gatherings
here   a table set with fruit pies galore
on another   sits a trussed and roasted pig
a mocking apple caught within his lonely jowls
eyeballing shirt-waisted ladies in their finery
smiling gents fisting cigars
guileless children playing as children do
their inheritances assured
while treed men swing with hung heads
mouths stuffed full
sunlight shines through necklaced trees
gracing a Sunday southern picnic

---

* *We Charge Genocide: The Crime of Government Against the Negro People* is a paper accusing the United States government of genocide based on the UN Genocide Convention. This paper was written by the Civil Rights Congress (CRC) and presented to the United Nations at meetings in Paris in December 1951.

III

Since 1860, a century of sanctioned schools* for Indians
Ninety plus ten sites littered the land
Uncle Sam's brainchild to salvage red babies
Kill the Indian, save the man
Impound native words; foreclose the sacred
Comb God into shorn locks
Make them weep for blood culture, then trek the tears
Ten little Indians
And then there were none

* Native American Boarding Reservation schools began in the late 1800's
The purpose? to deculturate the Native American children living on reservations and assimilate them into American culture

IV

Amidst plantations they've set aflame
The enslaved throw off their manacles
Freedom's the destination   no matter the terrain
Drink the machete, wear the whip
Skin the Master, sip his sweat
Oh, *Maroons**
Feral, fierce--- free!

* *Maroons* were escaped enslaved peoples

V

~ after Naomi Shihab Nye's "Blood"

Never dismiss the power of the King's English
My bourgeois father would say.
A dark urban monarch,
He lulled many to slaughter with multi-syllabic words
My Father, a verbal grim reaper
Preferred language over guns or box cutters

When I was young and militant, he wore his Negro-tude like new money
Strutting word by polished word
Laughed at queries posed to him:
Where on the map is Negro-land? I asked.

He dreamed of eating watercress sandwiches with
Alabama housewives at Woolworth's
While I preferred the proletariat comforts of fatback and hog maws
When African repatriation pressed the agenda forward
He claimed Negroes were non-returnable items with
Melanin being a firmly affixed label

Father's family migrated to Illinois from Mississippi
By pocketing the North Star[1] and
'Following the drinking gourd'[2]
Harnessing energy loosed by its brilliance—its light giving hope, spawning new futures
Hope like an elixir everyone drank
Hope as knowledge harvested from abundant fields

If we returned to Africa tomorrow, how would we thrive?
Homeless strange fruit[3], we now be
Tragic human produce with dwarfed and aimless roots
Plucked from our life source
Worked and discarded, re-hung on trees
These days, Father and I recoil at the news:
Commoditized prisoners as stock

Father shakes his fist in the air so hard
His diplomas quiver
The frames slide down the wall like beads of sweat
What is the point? He asks with furrowed brow,
Of listening to ancestors with restless legs?

We, who have lost our mothers,[4] lost our way?

[1] Enslaved Blacks used the North Star to guide them north
[2] Words from a folk song about the Underground Railroad during slavery
[3] "Strange fruit" referenced Blacks who were lynched and hung from trees
[4] Lost your mother: a term referencing Blacks whose ancestors were captured in Africa and sent to the New World as slaves

VI

O, Henrietta Lacks Lacks Lacks*
Was poor and Black Black Black
Had advanced cancer cancer cancer
John Hopkins hospital gave her flak flak flak
They probed her body body body
She finally died died died
Her feisty cells cells cells
Were kept alive alive alive
Praise be to HeLa HeLa HeLa
The cell industry thrives thrives thrives
But, Henrietta's descendants, struggle to survive survive survive

---

* The multimillion-dollar cell culture industry was spawned by the original tumor cells of Henrietta Lacks (HeLa)

VII

Twas 1884 at the Berlin
Convention   not an African
Person present, nary a one
Mother Africa lay splayed out
On the table   writhing
(She was) sliced and diced along
lines of colonial convenience

An ecstatic King Leopold drew
Straws for the Congo   materializing his dreams
Of tiny chocolate hands*
Clapping

---

* Antwerp, Belgium is the chocolate capital that produced severed chocolate hands ~reminiscent of King Leopold II's practice of forcing the Congolese into labor and severing hands if production quotas of rubber or ivory were unmet.

VIII

Bring them to their knees with a strong vodoun.
Those that dare rob Haitian voices of sweet song
Who needs guns? We fight the French with our brains.

Tend Master's crops, nurse his young. By night,
stolen kisses. By day, angry lashes.
Bring them to their knees with a strong vodoun.

Doctor M* descends from the Hills with herbs
Strong enough to fell oxen and men
Who needs guns? We fight the French with our brains.

Dark sultry hips entice from the cane fields
Make the foreman dance like winged cattle
Bring them to their knees with a strong vodoun.

The plans to ignite each farm with black magic
revealed to the French by one tortured girl
Who needs guns? We'll fight the French with our brains.

The French were sent spinning by another
tactician. Toussaint's groundwork set by M
Bring them to their knees with a stealth vodoun
Who needs guns? We fought the French with our brains.

---

* Makandal was known as "Doctor" for his medicinal knowledge of herbs; he fled slavery for the hills in Haiti inhabited by other Maroons

IX

First freed nation; first in impoverishment
Haiti banished the Imperialists
Wrestled the heavy chains from around their own necks
Said France and the US, 'Haiti will pay'
For 100 years, Haiti paid ransom
What price freedom? $21 billion francs
A debt the world knows is owed Haiti by France

X

Boukman and Cecile dance as rain clouds beckon,
Dance atop black pig hide, an offering a dance
Commemorating their allegiance. Never captivate Haitians.

We gather, comparing atrocities
Wrought by those with the keys to the chains, while
Hougan and Mambo dance under the rain.

In those infamous Gator Woods, the storm
Sparks souls to battle. Prayers rage on and
A blood-let cry: Never enslave Haitians.

Staccato drums temper a high pig squeal.
When clouds clear, the pig's head's jammed on a stick,
The high priest and priestess orbit again.

History alone will decide which dance
Was revolutionary, meanwhile, woe
To those who dare shackle a Haitian.

The first in liberation in the west
Now, among nations, the poorest. Visions
Of Boukman and Cecile dancing magic
So, all will know: Never chain Haitians.

Note: Bois Caïman (lit. Cayman 1 Woods; Kreyòl: Bwa Kayiman) is the site of the vodou ceremony presided over by Boukman Dutty and Cecile Fatiman on August 14, 1791. It is widely accepted as the starting point for the Haitian Revolution.

XI

these French West Africans so
keen to save face
they do not say "my home is
afire
my family must
flee   I am terrified"

instead

they smile   they kiss ~ ~ twice
they

run

        we were simply visiting   when
        it   all fell   a p a r t   the year 2000
        Abidjan, CI

        coupe d'etat #1

        then   coupe d'etat #2

        a   warning   shot!
        man-sized   pictures of
        general Gui   spring up   outside buildings
        in banks   in stores   in the airport   in hotels

scent of the century

eau d'resistance

smoldering rebels   burn
government incensed   bodies
smoking   garbage and
bullets   are   everywhere

Silenced neighbors pass
in the streets and   whisper
the word of the day is *hoard*
food   water   matches   flashlight   batteries   gasoline
a transistor radio is
silver   guns are   gold

peer through shades   see
young boys cradling M16s like
Gucci   book   bags

        fearing the checkpoint soldiers' hungry bullets
        we   grease a   safer route with   cash

        we dim lights   extinguish music
        we mattress the floor
        huddle to hush the
        24-hour rat-tat-tatting

        Screams from next door   I cannot   forget
        faces and people   I cannot   name or find

        the date   bodies retrieved from the swamp
        I   can not
        re live re see
        any of   it

        except   on   the   page

name the conflict is
South versus North
tribal origin versus Ivoirite

it's all in who you   worship   worship   worship

Note: The first Civil War in *Cote d'Ivoire* began September, 2002 between the Muslim North and the Christian South ostensibly over the issue of national identity

XII

Detroit, my hometown, has gone up in flames*
The targets are places that have bled the poor dry
Watch shacks and shackles burn without shame

Stores leeching profits go first, no one's killed
The owners dwell in suburbs far from the fires
Detroit, my hometown, is going up in flames

Molotov cocktail throwers brandish their skills
Scores of fires overpower under cover of night
Watch shacks and shackles burn without shame

Why torch one's own home? The wealthy exclaim
Though, some death trap tenement buildings should be lit
Detroit, my hometown, please don't perish in flames

Sheltering in place, Dad wryly proclaims,
"No looter will get past my gun!" What gun?
Watch shacks and shackles burn with no shame

Dousing the rage becomes a waiting game
Martial law is declared; tanks roll down our street
My hometown, my hometown, has gone up in flames
Watching, I see shacks and shackles burn without shame

****

Postscript: Concrete rivers snake through this urban wasteland. My tears overflow in the express-lanes but the cars will never return. Say nice things about this once-vibrant jungle where singers smoldered. Shells of buildings smatter the landscape like old pockmarks. The memory stench burns and I feel the sad convulsive urge to leave as I did 50 years ago after the damned riots.

Note: During the summer of 1967, the Detroit riots were fueled by police brutality, injustice and economic inequality

XIII

A visit to
the Deep South
interviewing for
a place to reside and work and
Hang up my travel-weary hat

Nature's statuesque roadside greeters
Catch my eye   *Hello*
Tall dignified portals of Southern life
Wave hospitably as I drive by

Vibrant foliage dazzles
Fronds of rambunctious green
Rosettes of tawny orange
Gold-streaked leafage
Cover branches that
Some decades back   groaned from the weight of
Twisting wretched fruit

Rancid nectar dripping dark
Seeping deep into musty souls
Impregnating surly root formations.
Now, sighting those magnificent trees
I marvel: such a rich fertilizer: *blood*.

XIV

I will not touch this wound   will not   I've taped my hands at night worn mittens and gloves   created internal distractions to stay as far the hell away   from myself so the hurts could crust and scab over   I am a Black mother who told both children at their becoming ages what it meant to be a Black in America; as they left the Cute age, transitioned to the Intimidating age, & arrived at the Dangerous age—America's categories for Black youth—I read the little black book to them at night *How to Be Black and Stay Alive*—my girl included—the book told you to look a grownup in the eye; to neither smirk nor shirk nor grin when spoken to; stressed the importance of enunciating and articulating the King's English every day; to respect their elders; to neither lie nor cheat; to say 'yes sir' to an officer; and understand that milk is a food not a beverage

when my son was a phd at U Chicago*, he organized a protest group—U Chicago having closed their Trauma Unit forcing many South Siders to bleed to death en route to an ER across town; Miz O was then administrator—the group leafleted, held talks, picketed, engaged and enraged the University for years   someone sent me a YouTube video of my son's arrest at one protest   Chi town cops surrounded him   he asked that they call the University because the protest was sanctioned   he used the safe word   those pigs took my 77-inch baby down   face down   then opened ranks the camera showed him on his face on the ground handcuffed   my heart flash froze   I tried to squeeze my body up into that phone and shove aside those cops slip off his manacles and say, "get up, Baby. Mama's here."   this drama plays on repeat in my head a zillion times each day each night Trayvon Martin / Eric Garner / Sean Bell / Michael Brown / Alton Sterling made the news for walking or running or speaking for saying nothing or breathing or simply being Black   and human silent tears well and crest inside my pain is a wrapped box no one wants to open the anti-gift   I am all Black mothers to all Black daughters and sons birthing them growing them launching them into the world to fight social wrongs or die trying   their exit wounds wound me   linger deep crust over   taut tough scars I point to with Black motherpride this scab that scab

"there, those be my sons"

* The U Chicago Med Center broke ground on a new trauma center 9/2016— two years after my son received his doctorate

XV

Put the word out   on the street we're out of asylum*

finished   we're not stocking asylum this season   there'll be no safe harbor here

if you were looking for justice / equality / a listening hand / freedom from persecution—we used to carry all those things but no more!

asylum was getting *way* too popular!   *everybody* wanted it!   we couldn't keep it on the shelves   it got out of hand

anyway   we won't be offering asylum under current management

you ask—*is there* anywhere *one can find some asylum these days? under the table? for above market price? You say you just want a whiff?*

well you might try our neighbor to the north—they may have a small amount of vintage asylum   left   i wouldn't advise trying our southern neighbors they're liable to tell you *si, como no? asylum* then try and interest you in some AR-15s smuggled from here to there

---

* Central American asylum seekers on the U.S. southern border struggle to escape gang violence and persecution in Guatemala, Honduras and El Salvador

XVI

How does a gun smell
Pressed against your head?
Smoky/dark—like meat left to rot?
Sweaty/hot—like fear?
Am I dead? Am I smoked?
The man from outofnowhere steps to you
Presses cold metal in your face
Icing ironic your pacifism
He makes an offer you dare not refuse
Your car or your life or
Your car then your life
A confused demand lost in translation
In a place where stakes heighten fast
Neighborhood pigs abound
Neighbors packing guns abound
Free range and dangerous
Black movement enrages police and alt righters
Douse your hoodie
Your phone, toss your loosies, fix your car lights,
Don't hold no knife no pipe no shower head no toy gun,
Hands high, don't talk, don't run and
Don't be in the wrong place (like home)
No need to breathe,
They wasting you anyway

XVII

scab-girl come over   scab-girl come over
come over come over   sit and stay awhile

your body aches are not fictitious
they dwell not solely within your mind

hidden sores seep through to bone
belied by vigilant scars

with the right incantations
our soul traumas fill massive tomes

don't pick those crusts just now
lest blood drip to your toes

and shameless demons arise
thirsting thirsting for more and more

scab-girl come over   scab-girl come over
come over   come over

spill the tea upon sacred dirt
not just   that witnessed   or heard
but   what you read and wrote

dribble secrets that hiss and sputter
under the smoking lens of truth

we'll dissect your stories bone
by tendon   by nerve

XVIII

he wants us all
gone from Amerikkka
purge all 52
Main Streets   there's a
main street in every
state your name for the record and
your color state your
color me paranoid color me
afraid of civil war
I would gladly leave this country
voluntarily than stay and be forced to leave this earth
if all the colored people
black and brown go
back where we came from it will
be a pretty bleak bland
picture BLAXIT*
all spices are coming with us along with
sweet potatoes / peanuts / mac'n cheese / ribs
all greens are coming also watermelon / peaches / mangos
all berries   coconut/ pineapple/ avos
pears can stay   coffee will come and all manner of liquor and
    whiskey
we harvest chocolate   so it's coming
gone by sundown
goners we will be if we stay
I don't have a country but no
matter I will find something
you-all will have
no music it's
coming with us jazz
and rap and soul and be-bop and
blues   always blues

you all can have country
western and classical
we're taking Beyonce, Toni Morrison,
Oprah, Rihanna you
can have Kanye
Wakanda is us
all black inventions will come like ice cream / peanut butter /
potato chips / guitars / traffic lights / elevators / refrigerators /
staplers / fire extinguishers / lawn mowers / baby buggys

we'll take all living poets of color from
the beat period on
Pete Seeger was wrong: this land IS your stolen land
enriched by our blood

* BLAXIT signifies the exit of Black people from America

XIX

And because she was a rest
less babe wanting more
than to march and
sing "stand by me"

And because her
hometown burned and
Dexter Avenue
smoldered
from spent
cocktails

And because the betrayal
leading to
Malcolm X's death razed
her fledgling dreams

And because Vietnam
was a slow
inferno and
veteran carcasses roamed
the streets

And because darkness gave cover to
the Black Cat skulking with
urban calm

She hailed that Cat
threw her leg
over its wild part   and
clutched its warm
recesses

And because they rode
with revolutionary
wile into
the city's bowels then rose
up through its consciousness like Icarus

And because the spirits of Fanon and
Lumumba exalted
them with a chorus of
berets: all ways the people

And because the Cats cross-haired power and
mastered the
photo op: the FBI took note—igniting
a battle

And because JE Hoover smoked those
Black
Cats
from
the
sky
Cat hair and claws were
everywhere

Note: The FBI developed COINTELPRO a counterintelligence program from the 1950s used to disrupt and destroy the Black Panther Party

XX

What happens to the man behind bars?
The Constitution's a document   great at
safeguarding freedoms for individuals who
rate and   for corporations given *individual* status
We lease prisoners to factories and farms to harvest crops
until their hearts burst or their limbs erupt
We lash convicts to fishing boats 'til dry land's a
Distant memory
Flimsy weed infractions entrap those too poor to afford counsel
While sky-high bond/bail and bounty ensnare
These laments are pleasing lyrics for holders of private prison stock
The 13th amendment's writ: Slavery's abolished*
Except for those chained to Capitalism

---

*The thirteenth amendment to the Constitution abolished slavery except as punishment for a crime (incarceration)

XXI

At work   this Black girl foments fear   her staff
hide and quiver   her footsteps
quake walls   on a good day
her dreadlocked aura   resets office clocks and
tilts previously-level paintings

a befuddled communication
coach   jars of Hydroquinone* and smiling
exercises that display her pearly
whites are all salvage
plans to protect
her co-workers from her
Neon Black
Body

*Hydroquinone~ a skin bleaching cream

XXII

no one   no one   no one
is coming to save us
you garble words in the
morning served up by your grisly
nightmares: *cash in your CDs*
walk away from the mortgage
whatever shithole country will take you and
masquerade as your new home
fashion u a pillow on the beach
strap you into a new culture
erase the disaster that has been America
run   run   run   while there is time   still

no one is coming   no one is coming   are you leaving
you poll your friends   your loves
are you ready   are you packing
you've read about the stadiums in Pinochet's Chile
about Argentina's *desaparecidos*
about the Khmer Rouge's search for those wearing glasses and
you stew at the news with knowing disbelief
it can happen anywhere   look at Turkey
it's unlikely to go down following some official notice
you will have no time to tweet or text your homies
the Jews did not put signs in their store windows—"closed for the
   summer"
natives on the Trail did not have time to dry buffalo jerky
no one will aid us
the signs are all aligned   that it will happen   not how
will martial law be enacted?
will calls go out on social media like Rwanda's historic urgings of
pest control?

no one aided the Croatians/ the Tutsis/ /the Rohingyas
Dr Cress Welsing never lied
thirty years ago   she warned
white men fear their genetic
disappearance   disappearing
us is their remedy
and who will come   who will come   who will come to our aid?

XXIII

Lupita speaks in tongues, hosts
ravenous haunts—my second
child of three, my medium
in the middle   quiet to the point
of translucence. Bewitching
girl of icy dead-
patience   asks:
can Papa Wilbur stay for dinner?

tonight, winds claw the moon,
fierce chill cuts to bone.
grandfather's father was
Jim-Crow-lynched,
dismembered and burned.
our broken bough returns for feast.
an amalgam of char and ooze,
he stands near Lupita, cradling his skull.
the two exhale as I assent
sure—I say—sure   and
set an extra plate.

XXIV

I come from a line of rage-full folk
Rage-filled   Raging   Full-on   full-up enraged people
I do get it honest

ours is a line of rage-full folk with
the power to flee
whippings from the overseer
later, the lynching parade
now, flee the gun chastising us for the
busted taillight
courtesy of cortisol*
a chromosomal microdot hosting
that chemical keeping us on high alert   causing
sugar diabetes
high blood
cancer
stroke
court-a-soul   it
wounds the womb
inflames the blood
perimeters gut fat   it
speeds the mind
a self-wrought PTSD
elixir of choice for the hunted
every adult POC in the USA has loads

genetic rage

mine is a line of rage-full folk
lines of waiting folk enraged but calm
waiting to work
waiting for the next shoe drop
rage passing through generations like electricity
sparking a few   burning out many

echoes of slavery steeped in our genes
rendering us
eternally vigilant   internally restless
we all sleep with both eyes open

* Studies show that serum cortisol (the stress hormone) output increases with repeated exposure to episodes of racial discrimination

Acknowledgments

Grateful acknowledgement to the editors of the following journals and anthologies, in which poems in this collection first appeared in their original form with an alternate title:

"Picnic" (Roman Numeral II), "Anatomy of a Scar" (Roman Numeral XIV), and "Bois Caiman Ceremony" (Roman Numeral X) were first published in the anthology *50/50: Poems & Translations by Women over 50* (QuillsEdge Press).

"Until Further Notice: Asylum is Out of Stock" (Roman Numeral XV) appeared in *New Verse News* (9/17/19).

"Blaxit" (Roman Numeral XVIII) was first published in *Kosmos Quarterly: journal of global transformation* (Spring, 2020).

Praise for *Picking Scabs from the Body History*

Dr. Joanne Godley's *Picking Scabs from the Body History* is a collection of poems whose pulse is powered by its ability to both document and archive the complexity of the African diasporic experience. Polyvocal in narration, *Picking Scabs from the Body History* considers the blatant and pernicious consequences of slavery and its enduring legacy, most clearly manifested through the dispossession of a people's culture and selfhood. With its increasing zoom from the landscape of history and into the marrow of family stories, Dr. Godley brings the abstract natures of justice and injustice to eye level—it is in these moments that the reader sees the inextricability of the personal and the political. It is in these moments that the reader also witnesses the brilliance of survival and self-possession. Unflinching in its indictment of the human condition, one of this collection's greatest strengths is its honesty, one that is prismatic in its manifold expressions of exactitude, lyricism, passion, and erudition. This is the type of honesty that at its core, invites us to examine how we might hold the value of human life and dignity with all that it is owed—these poems challenge us to imagine and model a more radical, selfless, inclusive, and incandescent form of love.

> —Yalie Kamara, author of *When the Living Sing*
> and *A Brief Biography of My Name*

From the opening scene in a child's library through historical and personal locations that remind, inform, and gut punch with stark imagery and pared-down language, Joanne Godley's *Picking Scabs from the Body History* tracks the movement of racialized bodies through American history. A fiercely attuned chronicle of the violence and collective trauma of these United States, its "indelible truths" enact corporeality and rage through the thrum of rhythm and repetition and the lush compounding of sounds. It digs down, mapping through language the "surly root formations" of our very foundation. Through these poems we are shown back to ourselves and beseeched to "erase the disaster that has been America" to "run run fly   while there is time   still." A masterful chapbook and absolute necessary read.

—Elizabeth J. Colen, author
What Weaponry and *The Green Condition*

About the Author

Joanne Godley is a practicing physician, poet and writer whose work is informed by social injustices. She is a native of Detroit residing in Alexandria, Virginia. She is convinced she is a descendant of nomads because traveling is one of her great passions (along with art collecting, salsa dancing and cycling). She spent time working in Africa as a Peace Corps medical officer.

Godley's lyric memoir was a finalist for the Kore Press Memoir contest and the Sunshots Press Prose Contest, and it received honorable mentions in the Deborah Tall Lyric Essay Book contest and the National Woman's Book Association Contest. She completed an online novel writing certification program through Stanford University. Her first novel was ranked finalist in Kimbilio's annual novel writing contest.

Three of her poems were published in an anthology. A flash creative nonfiction piece was recently published in the *Kenyon Review* blog and a flash *noir* fiction piece appears on the Akashiac Press blog, *Mondays are Murder*. Godley attended the Bread Loaf Writer's Conference in 2018 and the Kenyon Writers Workshop in 2019. She is a member of the Women's Fiction Writing Association, the Author's Guild and the NWBA.

About The Poetry Box®

The Poetry Box® is a boutique publishing company in Portland, Oregon, which provides a platform for both established and emerging poets to share their words with the world through beautiful printed books and chapbooks.

Feel free to visit the online bookstore (thePoetryBox.com), where you'll find more titles including:

The Dichotomy Between Light & Dark by Michael B. Carroll Jr.

Surreal Expultion by D.R. James

Like the O in Hope by Jeanne Julian

Shadow Man by Margaret Chula

What She Was Wearing by Shawn Aveningo Sanders

Womanhood & Other Scars by Rebecca Smolen

Many Sparrows by donnarkevic

Gospel Gone Blues by Jimmie Ware

(good cape weather) by Wes Jordans

The Screaming Silence by Lanser Howard

Staring Down the Tracks by Julia Paul

and more . . .

www.ingramcontent.com/pod-product-compliance
Lightning Source LLC
LaVergne TN
LVHW012131070526
838202LV00056B/5953